The Scenic Road

Melisa Sandoval

Presentation by *BookLeaf Publishing*

Web: www.bookleafpub.com

E-mail: info@bookleafpub.com

ISBN: 9789357747615

First edition 2023

This book is dedicated to my friends and family. Thank you for always being there for me.

ACKNOWLEDGEMENT

My younger sister, Yareli, who has always been my biggest supporter. Always reassures me and pushes me to try my best. <3

My Fiancé, Daniel Rodriguez, who has always been understanding, encourages me and supports me to follow my dreams. <3

To the Readers - Thank You for taking a chance on me reading my very first book. <3

PREFACE

These poems came to life based on how I felt and viewed things on a personal level and seeing others around me. I did my best to try and word them in the best way possible to feel and capture the message in each one.

I hope you enjoy reading them as much as I have enjoyed writing them.

Let the road trip begin.

Lost.

I have been feeling lost for a long time.
Trying to find the person I am meant to be.
It seems like I'm stuck in a body with a mind
that isn't mine.
Making me feel like I am trapped inside.
Constantly fighting to set myself free.

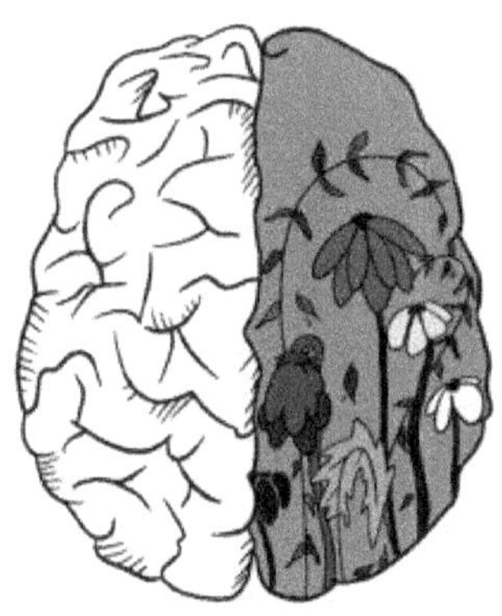

The Worst Emotion

What is the worst emotion a human can feel?
Nothing.
Numbness.
Emptiness.
Not being able to show how you truly feel,
who you truly are.

Glimpses of Euphoria

Sometimes people need a break from life.
The constant chaos can get to our body and
head.
We tend to escape to the mountains to yet once
again feel alive.
Sometimes we tend to feel like our dreams are
dead.
We stare down at the city view
contemplating what we can change to feel bliss.
Really tired of always feeling blue.
We begin to think of our dreams and reminisce.
Feeling motivated,
Staring up at the beautiful moon,
Thinking maybe we can start living our dream.
We set goals to complete in six months.
Typically by June.
We are at the top feeling excited;
We just wanna scream.
It is now time to drive back down to the city.
Sadly, nothing yet has changed in our sorrowful
reality.

Empty and Bare

We all have those days where our lives feel
empty and bare.
Desperately longing to change.
Wanting to escape those overwhelming thoughts
that somehow makes us feel paralyzed.
All the pressure we face.
People crowding our heads with screaming
thoughts that won't go away.
Saying we can do better.
Often questioning our existence and purpose.
Thinking maybe we haven't done enough.
Yet we've come pretty far from where we used
to be.
It takes time to once again visualize the bigger
picture
that makes the little bits of progress worth it.
We all are worthy of the life we were given.
Have hope that sooner or later you will bloom at
your given time.
The truth is we never stop blooming,
even if at times we do feel
empty and bare.

Timeline

Age 16, part-time job
Age 18, acceptance letters
Age 22, earn a degree
Age 23, "dream job"
Age 24, six-figure salary
Age 25, married
One year later, kids
...
Age 65, retirement

Now ask yourself one question,
Were you living or just existing?

Society can really mess with your mind if you
let it.
It will give you a timeline.
It will tell you all these different norms
and rules that you need to follow.
If you continue letting society guide your life
you will never truly feel fulfilled.
You will feel like you are living for other people
and before you realize it,
life will be passing you by.
Don't let them give you a timeline.
Don't build your life based on society's thoughts.

Do what your heart tells you
Or else you will continue to feel miserable.
It is never too late to break through.

The Blindsided Journey

Many times we can't see what's ahead of us.
Making us feel scared,
Yet curious.
It's okay to feel tired.
It's okay to take a little break.
But we must not stop moving forward.
We have to continue till we reach our next pit
stop.
And just hope for the best.
None of us know what's ahead.
We all just roam and wander through this
blindsided journey called life.

Reminder

Smiling slowly seems impossible as everything
around you is
shattering and falling apart.
Here's a little reminder.
Pause,
Breathe,
Then press play when you feel ready
to keep moving forward.

Breathe

Being surrounded by nature feels like a beautiful
therapy session.
It's just you and the fresh breeze
from the trees
that help you breathe
and think more clearly.

The Temporary Flame

Our candles won't stay lit forever.
The flame can become dim at any given
moment.
So don't let time pass you by
without doing the things you love to do.
Take risks,
Take a chance,
And most importantly,
Live your life each day as if it were your last.

The Lonely Shadow

Alone is what my shadow always looks like,
Wandering through the brightest days.
Slowly becoming myself as darkness falls.

A Moment of Peace

Breathing and sitting here on the oceanic sand.
Seeing the ocean and hearing the waves
peacefully crash.
Away from the city.
Away from the noise.
Privileged to be empty-minded
Without having to make any choice.
At that moment nothing else really matters.
It is just you and your dreams.
Not having to face reality.

Patience

Butterflies are truly amazing.
In the early stages of their life,
They drag themselves through the world.
Trying to stay alive living on the ground below.
Just like humans, they go into hiding,
And when their timing is right,
they create a cocoon, camouflaging themselves
from the world,
and slowly transform.
And when ready, they rip through the cocoon
they were once safely in,
They break free and fly with their
bright vibrant colored wings.
Now, instead of dragging themselves through
ground,
They are soaring high through the sky.

I like to think they represent how we feel
in the early stages of our lives.
Dragging ourselves through the ground.
Until we decide to focus on ourselves,
We too transform.
Then when the timing is right,
When we are ready,
we too break free and spread our wings.

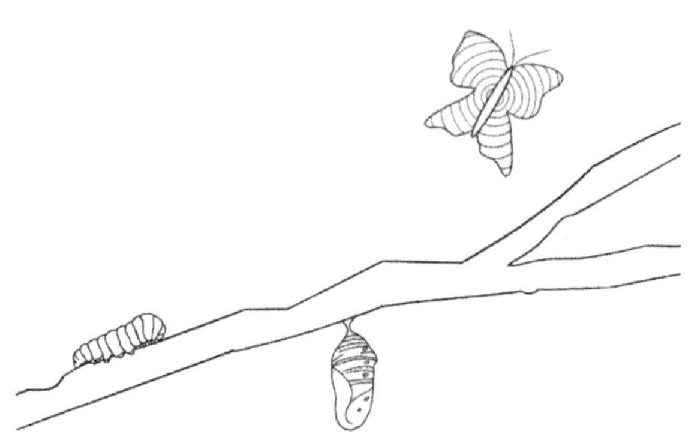

True Love

Many say that true love doesn't exist
in this modern world.
Often times longing for it to arrive at their door.
But in reality every time they look in the mirror,
they fail to see their eyes are the doorway to
their beautiful soul,
A soul they had not yet explored.
Finding out they had true love all along within.

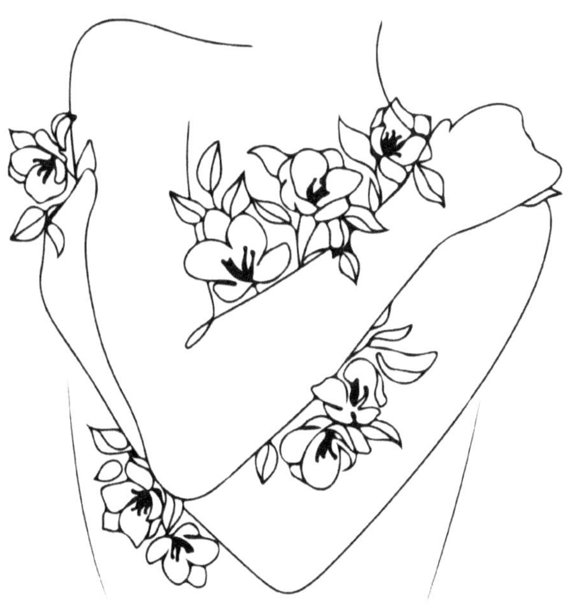

The Wandering Soul

Allow your soul to wander through your imagination.
It will help you find yourself.

Your Story

Your life is your story.
You are the main character.
Choose the story you would like to write.
For you only have one story to leave behind
before reaching the unpredictable finish line.

Time Stands Still

Life doesn't seem to slow down
even when we really need it to,
But when I lay on your chest,
everything in the external world disappears,
And it is just you and me,
and the rhythm of your heartbeat.
It is my peaceful place in this chaotic galaxy.

Giving Love a Chance

People around us will have different views on
love.
Some will give advice depending on what they
have gone through.
Many have walls up and don't fully trust.
It is no surprise as people try to avoid getting
hurt once more.
You too at some point believed that motto
and promised yourself to not ever trust blindly.
To never get fooled once again.
After all, it is more safe that way.

Until that moment comes
and you cross paths with the love of your life.
And all of those promises you made to yourself
when your heart was once hurt,
All of a sudden, inevitably dissolve.
You can try to not fall too deeply,
But it is no use.
For it is simply a strong feeling that overtakes
your heart,
mind and soul completely.
And to your surprise,
you realize you are not broken like you once
believed to be.

You come to realize your heart can feel again.
You feel an electrifying connection when you
lock hands.
Something you hadn't felt before.
You are happy.
And the wounds your heart once felt,
now feel mended.
You are delighted to have given love a chance
And did not ignore.
For you now feel more alive than ever before.

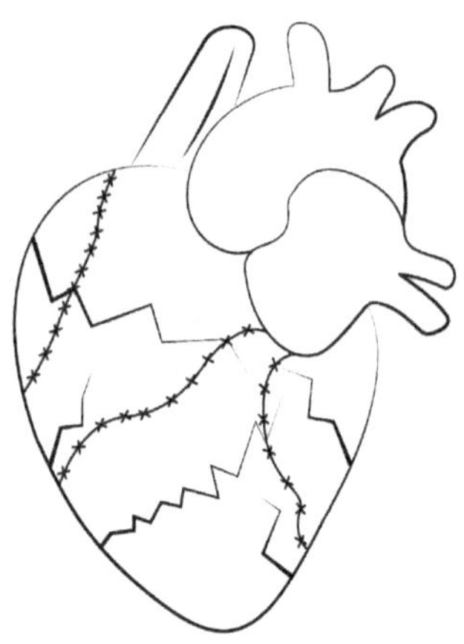

Dandelion

Pick a Dandelion.
Close your eyes.
Think of all the negative thoughts holding you
back,
Take a deep breath,
And blow them away into the wind.

Your Eyes

Hiking up the mountain hill.
The beautiful view up there looks so unreal.
Surrounded by green and yellow flowers,
A little lake and lots of beautiful trees.
It is golden hour.

Once the honey light kissed your eyes,
I once again felt hypnotized.
Taking in every detail,
I am in awe and mesmerized.

Only this time it was different.
I came to realize those beautiful eyes are not
only green,
But around the iris, there are also glimpses of
light hazel brown.
Just like the color of nature's scenery in the
spring,
When I stare into your beautiful eyes,
it's like everything else around me disappears.
When I stare into your eyes,
I feel love.
I feel peace.
I see home.

The Road

It is easy for others to judge your life.
Pointing and laughing at you,
not knowing all the obstacles you've had to
overcome
along that long, curvy road.
What they lack in knowing is,
the destination is not yet reached,
as those close-minded people choose to blindly
think.
But one day they'll be able to see
All that you've been working on and achieved.
No more judgments.
No more laughs.
Just hypocritical faces watching me.
I have made it at last.

No Longer Lost.

I no longer feel as if there's a missing piece.
I no longer feel numb.
I'm no longer in a sleep state.
At last, I woke up.

My heart is now beating,
and dreams turned into reality.

I'm no longer just breathing,
but truly living.
And I must say,
it's quite riveting.

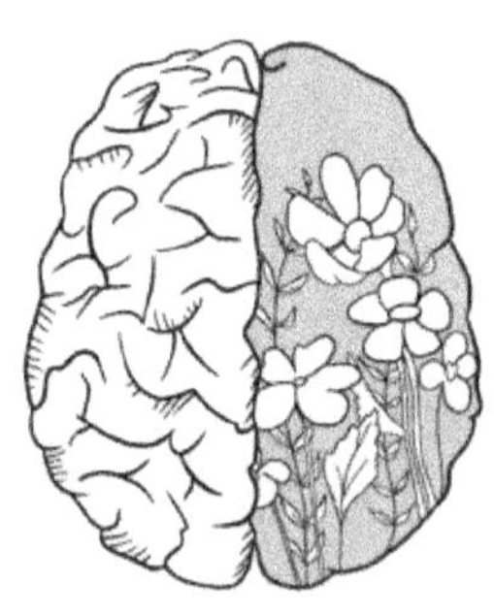